A GRINGO LIKE ME
Jennifer L. Knox

A Gringo Like Me: Poems
SECOND EDITION
Copyright © 2007 Jennifer L. Knox
(First edition was © 2005 Jennifer L. Knox, published by Soft Skull Press)

Cover painting: Charles Browning "The Greenest Tree in the Land of the Free," 2002. Charles Browning is represented by Schroeder Romero, New York, NY. For more information, see www.schroederromero.com.

Cover design: Charles Orr

Published by Bloof Books
www.bloofbooks.com

Bloof Books are distributed to the trade via Ingram, Baker & Taylor, and other wholesalers. Individuals may purchase them direct from our website, from online retailers such as Amazon.com, or request them from their favorite bookstores. (Please support your local independent bookseller whenever possible.)

ISBN: 978-0-6151-6144-0

For Sean

MIGHTY, MIGHTY PRIMATE: RECONSIDERED

Ladies and gentlemen, *Mighty, Mighty Primate*
is a great, great
movie.

Initially, we all had our
doubts, but it's
great.

The part where I was lashed to the ship deck with chains in a typhoon
made me
cry.

And as the elected representative of giant apes everywhere,
I implore you, world leaders:
unplug

those spotlights in the parking lot,
send the helicopter squadrons
home.

Remember the lessons of *Mighty, Mighty Primate*:
Whenever missionaries crash land in the Himalayas, a giant ape
will feed them.

Whenever a crack team of Chinese explorers
loses their footing and plunges into a cavernous gorge, a giant ape
will catch them.

Thank you. Now I'd like to give you all an opportunity
to behold the wonder of my incredible nip
ples.

Love Blooms at Chimsbury after the War

After a round of croquet in the garden, Pimpton
dropped dead with our lunch in his hands. Then Babette
dropped dead under her wide-brimmed straw hat. Poncey
dropped dead, then Alice, then Tuckles. The sweep dropped
dead from his perch on the roof, then Yappy, our cocker,
dropped dead under a bush. We peered out the gate, watched
the town dropping dead: the butcher all bloody, the bobby,
the old pony hitched to the dead iceman's ice cart
dropped dead. Then you dropped dead, sis, and I might've
too if not for a vision of young Harold Winter,
the vicar, drifting down on parachute strings:
"I fear it's all my fault," he laughs easily.
Our children take to the trees every summer
while swallows rain down like overripe plums.

OF THE FLOCK

God
help us.
We're just not that bright

but we put on a good show:
the endless preening
and chirping in all the right places.

Windows
are unfathomable, though—
cover our cages
and we go *Nightie night*!

Double that dumbness
at the doctor's office,
waiting and waiting
atop piles of old *Time* while

symptoms
swoop down on our itty bitty brains
(laryngitis, mange, mysterious
sores on our tiny white tongues)
driving a red otherness
up the shaft of our feathers.

When a door
slams somewhere
you'd think a tiger just yelled
Bang! the way we all puff up
and shudder.

Who
thought this place up, anyway?
The color, no TV, no water fountain.
Nothing to do but stare
at the frosted glass
separating us from reception
and our test results.

                    Only the old birds
with occasional outbursts
speak our minds—
What the hell's going on here?!—
and we titter
together
(the pregnant wren,
the narcoleptic cardinal,
the grackle with Tourette's)
                    as one bird.

                         All except the robin—
                         worried little robin—
                         with a shoebox on his lap
                         that he keeps opening
                         and peeking in
                         and cooing to
                                   a smaller bird inside:

                         Hold on
                         cheepcheep
                         hold on

THE LAWS OF PROBABILITY IN LEVITTOWN

I've been smoking so much pot lately,
I figure out what my poems are going to do
before I write them, which means when I finally
sit down in front of the typewriter…well…you know…

I moved back in with my parents,
and I'm getting really good at watching TV.
Soon as I saw the housewife last night on *Inevitable Justice*,
I knew her husband was the killer and I told her so and I was right.

Remember whenever Jamie Lee Curtis would come
on TV and we'd yell, *Hermaphrodite!* all happy? I maintain
her father, Tony, is an American treasure, and have prepared a mental
list of examples why, so should we meet again, my shit's backed up.

There were too many
therapists in the city—97% of all therapists
are certifiable ding-dongs by nature which is fine
if you live in Platteville, Nebraska, where there's only

like three therapists in the entire town
(the odds are in your favor) but if 10,000
therapists are lurching around the streets, chances are
1,000 will be 100% batshit nuts.

I had a choice between watching
Robert Frost talking about his backyard
on *Large American Voices* and Farrah Fawcett on *True Hollyweird*.
I chose Farrah, because I knew what was going to happen and I was right.

Here's something I've been trying
to work in: *10 rations = 1 decoration.*
What do you think? *10 monologues = 5 dialogues,*
10 millipedes = 1 centipede, .000001 fish = 1 microfiche…

I've got a million of those.
I wrote them down, back when I was
writing things down. But I've been thinking I should
tip the Domino's kid more than a buck on 14. Should I?

My Favorite Little Story

Fitzsimmons was expounding upon *Tales of the Genji*:
"The court was a den of intrigue, their love
letters one line long—not pages and pages
of boo hoo hoo as in *Wuthering Heights*."
And that reminded me of my own little story:

"Well you know the Japanese were regarded
as the finest craftsman of miniatures in the world—
every medium: porcelain, jade, marble, maple
and poetry, you name it. Plus they're the only race
able to sex baby chickens." I paused extravagantly there

allowing the weight of my aside to sink in, "To go
boy, girl, boy, etc.? Just by looking?!? Wow wee!"
and then as I was segueing into the ability of certain Bornean
tree tribes to distinguish one camouflaged iguana
from another at ten clicks, Augswell chimed in:

"They have schools for that now."
"For iguanas?"
"No, for sexing baby chickens. My dear niece
took a hiatus from her animal husbandry doctorate
just to intern at the Boise facility."

Sleep that night was unusually sweaty.
I didn't drift off so much as
drop, roughly and loudly, level by level
like a doomed oil barge through a red, rusty series of locks.
Then the dream: an eight-inch Japanese schoolgirl approaches my bed

hefting a life-sized plastic donkey over her head.
You can tell it's not her donkey from the way she
drops it, grunting, "Sex this, dummy."
I recognize her voice: it's Miko-chan, an old student of mine.
The years had really improved her English. Dramatically so.

DISTRESS CALL FROM THE CANYON

Dear reader, I am writing to you
from deep inside my own ass.
My head is, I mean. Lodged,
if you will. And it's dark. So
what should we talk about?
Huh. Well, I've always wanted
to go camping with my family
and enjoy it—leave off squabbling
over the front seat, the radio
and soda and crap and act like we
belong outside like real people for once
in our lives for Christ's sake.

I mean, to drift down a river,
sans shirt or shame! To start
fires, count the seconds between
thunder claps! And stars!
I spy Orion's boner, Pop—ha ha!
To call out in the night
from the treacherously narrow path
to the toilet amidst yellow eyes
and sticker bushes: *Help me, family!*
I am so lost! and then be
certain of the helicopters' swift
surges off their concrete launch pads—

of their spotlights carefully combing
through the tall, lonely pines as if I were
one of their metallic,
whirling own.

RETICENCE IN THE AFTERGLOW OF A POWERFULLY FRISKY FIT

I'm lounging on the sofa
fondling a battery-operated Shih Tzu—
alive with Oriental pleasure.
I'm rattling a bright orange bottle
of expired antibiotics.
I'm surrounded by fat men
in neoprene wet suits who're trying
to tip over a vending machine.
I'm screaming
"GIVE ME BACK MY WIG YOU SHITS!"
I'm taunting some wet, frightened
varmint under the woodpile—
the kids keep begging me to quit it.
I'm primping in peanut butter
pasties and a candycane g-string.
I'm making your socks say
profane things to Puerto Ricans.
I'm smelling something: big time.
I'm fingering an electric frosting machine.
I'm licking a pay phone—on accident.
I'm contemplating the gift
of cheese while vomiting all over
a skee-ball game, much to
the midway's chagrin.
I'm telling you about this idea
I have to cover my yard
with Hostess SnoBalls, the pink ones—
all over the lawn and up the tree trunks
like a neon Eskimo town.
I'm interrupting you
to tell you my idea
about covering my yard
with pink Hostess SnoBalls —
you were saying something
about a good idea you had for your own yard.
I'm apologizing
for interrupting you.

CRUISING FOR PROSTITUTES

Motherfucker. I just found out my boyfriend's a prostitute.
And we were saving up to go on a cruise.
I went and got all these brochures
from the travel agent on my lunch hour.
Billy introduced and that motherfucker never said,
"Steve, meet Chet—he's a prostitute."
I think I would've remembered that.
I met Chet's family once, and they all seemed
perfectly normal. Not like prostitutes
or people who'd encourage
their son to become a prostitute.

But now that I think back on it, he never seemed
like he was paying attention, and he never got
mad. I thought he was just
stupid. So now I don't know
shit: are we still
going out? Is he going
to keep on being a prostitute?
Did that motherfucker Billy
know? Does Chet's family
know? Who else
knows? Has he even looked at
any of the brochures I brought home?
So what's it going to be?
The Fun Ship or the Love Boat?

AVENUE OF THE AMERICAS

BUT YOU COULD BE THE TOAST OF THE ART WORLD, BROCK!
I yell in my bullhorn from atop a Big Apple tour bus at dawn
going 75 up 6th—gnats stinging my face like a sandstorm.
My best friend, Billy, is one lane away on the upper deck of his own Big A
and as we fly by Gray's Papaya and Edith Wharton's childhood
home, he answers: HOW CAN I WHEN YOU'RE PREGNANT
WITH MY BABY? Good one. Take this: BUT YOU'RE BIGGER
THAN THIS ONE-HORSE FISHING BURG, BROCK!
Both drivers run the light at 14th and the buses bounce like sea lions
through the deserted intersection. Billy and I know enough
to hold our coffees up so they won't spill.
When we sail past the Gap, we yell, as always:
SEND OUT YOUR ALIEN HOTPANTS!
                                      Windows, windows
breathe through their mouths as we tear by,
their minds empty as the back side of a mirror. BUT MY FATHER
WAS A HARPOONIST, AS WAS HIS FATHER BEFORE HIM!
Billy's bus clips the rearview off a sleeping El Dorado—*fwip!*
These are the salad mornings: up 16th, 17th, 18th
and nobody back at dispatch knows what glorious birds we are—
us two—pecking holes in the Tree of Great Things.
Our wives think we're mopping up at an all-night laundromat.
SO GO TO PARIS AND PAINT YOUR HEART OUT!
BUT DO IT FOR YOUR FATHER, BROCK!
AND YOUR FATHER'S FATHER, BROCK!
                                      Under the Empire:
the sun's gotten strong enough to chase itself
through the windows. There goes another rearview,
dumb-ass bird, cardboard box. WE'LL GET SHOT
FOR THIS ONE DAY! Billy yells and right then another bus—
definitely not a Big Apple—turns onto 6th, heading straight at us—
totally going the wrong way way too fucking fast and some freak show's
on the roof wearing a cape or a plastic garbage bag yelling into a bullhorn
but he's not saying anything about the island's native inhabitants
or the birthplace of Theodore Roosevelt or Tammany Hall
and especially not the Parisian art scene—this nut's just screaming—
full speed ahead.

HOT ASS POEM

Hey check out the ass on that guy he's got a really hot ass I'd like to see his ass naked with his hot naked ass Hey check out her hot ass that chick's got a hot ass she's a red hot ass chick I want to touch it Hey check out the ass on that old man that's one hot old man ass look at his ass his ass his old man ass Hey check out that dog's ass wow that dog's ass is hot that dog's got a hot dog ass I want to squeeze that dog's hot dog ass like a ball but a hot ball a hot ass ball Hey check out the ass on that bird how's a bird get a hot ass like that that's one hot ass bird ass I want to put that bird's hot ass in my mouth and swish it around and around and around Hey check out the ass on that bike damn that bike's ass is h-o-t you ever see a bike with an ass that hot I want to put my hot ass on that bike's hot ass and make a double hot ass bike ass Hey check out that building it's got a really really really hot ass and the doorman and the ladies in the information booth and the guy in the elevator got themselves a buttload of hot ass I want to wrap my arms around the whole damn hot ass building and squeeze myself right through its hot ass and out the other side I want to get me a hot ass piece of all eighty-six floors of hot hot hot hot ass!

MEKONG

They killed all the trees
to see inside the forest
Then the fog rolled in

THE ORIGIN OF STORIES IN THE KINGDOM OF PARROTS

I'm standing amidst the ruins of the Plaza de la Sirena
with my parrot, Dr. José Venegas, who I suspect
of being tapped into some collective
archetypal memory bank with a bazillion other parrots—
the way thimble jellyfish are with other thimble jellyfish.
He knows colors and can count to ten—*nine, eight...*

...but I'm not sleepy yet, haven't slept in days, keep wondering
what forces carved this valley of serape stalls,
Gila monsters and the Forbidden Dance of Love.
Tidal waves? Glaciers?

"You made it up," Venegas says,
then laughs like a crazy parrot.

"What do you know? You're just a dentist!" I snap.
Yet there's something about the way he says it
that makes me think I've forgotten something terribly
important—like I left the iron on in Cleveland
thirty years ago—and whenever I think I've forgotten
something terribly important, I remember this story
about a man who built a bridge across the Amazon:

his wife flung herself over the thready mesh of suspension
wires which by all accounts were metallurgical miracles—
like something out of *Time Machine*
which hadn't even been written yet
or maybe she got sick—I forget
what happened exactly and I don't remember
who told me the story, but in my mind the edges
of the scene are always white and smoky
like a Japanese painting: the wooden slats swinging in
and out of the fog, the man's brown beard,
his wife's frail wrists, and the Amazon feeling
its way along the basin below swiftly
as a blind man over a love letter in Braille.

"You got it all wrong again," interrupts the parrot.
"That was my cousin, Ed,

who also built the World's Greatest Sandwich.
His girlfriend was a hooker who one time drank Sterno…"
I grab his beak and wring it, "Shut up!"
Then he flaps away all pissy and gingerly lands
on one of the Plaza's famed man-eating ferns.

This is how we do each other.
He calls it "rounding up the strays."
I don't know why he does, or what to call it
myself but I do know a private detective
showed me photos of the doctor with a bazillion other parrots
eating green-gray clay off a cliff by the seaside:
it helps them digest poisonous nuts and such.

So one day I asked Venegas about the clay
and if I could tag along. He turned on me
like an inbred pit bull: "You remember
the Polish National Church where
your mom and dad got married?
Well they tore it down
and put up a video arcade,
but you've been AWOL so long now you'll never
learn how to push the buttons! Never!"

So we avoid any talk of clay, cliffs, or nuts.
But between you and me, friend,
I'm standing amidst the ruins of the Plaza de la Sirena,
another ice age's on the way, and even after
sixteen root canals, something tells me not to
trust the bird's
telepathic tales from the Buckeye State.

SMALL ON SUNDAY

We woke up under an overpass on I-90
(at least the underside looked like I-90)
in the front seat of a yellow toy car.

Some guy had shrunk us again
and penned us in with giant orange traffic cones.
We must've looked pretty damn stupid.

The cars above us sounded on their way
to see the Sleepy Hippo at His shrine
(and to be seen by the Hippo at His shrine)

and the cars sounded happy enough.
Good, God-fearing people, I thought.
Salt of the Earth, you added.

We'd left our plastic bag of underpants
on a picnic bench in Muncie, the last time
we'd brushed our teeth: we were on E.

So there was nothing to do but think
of all things we wouldn't do that day
like going to see the Sleepy Hippo at His shrine

(we'd heard about the crowds,
the crows, the flowers, and all
the presents left around His pen—

so why did we keep taking a rain check?
Why all this wandering into xenophobic fish frys
to awake minuscule in some jerkwater burg?)

nothing to do but wait for that guy to come back
and spirit us out from the cones
with his little black remote control box.

SPRING AND STILL SOME SHORT

We are four little lambs
made entirely of daisies
and today we are having a party

on top of the river—the Old Man's chest—
as he sneezes thawed fishes
and wheezes our shed underfleece.

Counting; start again; start counting
again: we tried arranging the hamrolls
kitty-corner to the cupcakes

as well as adjacent to the cheese—
but dem poor old hamrolls,
they just keep rollin' along.

And with only one plastic fork left,
we'll give the oxen a rain check
and tell the peahens: *Skedaddle!*

Deep in the crimped paper plates
of our hearts, daisies beneath the daisies
fade as the daisies make daisies and daisies...

Look deep in our green glass eyes
at the sties, and at the lop-
sided moths on our noses.

A Gringo Like Me

(Curtain up on empty western street: High noon. Tumbleweed rolls by.)

Sfx: prairie wind.

(Enter right, **RED FARBEN**, hero, on tiptoe with shush finger pressed to pursed lips.)

RED
The telegram said to meet the Carne Brothers here at noon.
Music: Begin violent cellos.
If there's one thing I despise, it's a tardy outlaw.

(Enter left **CARNE BROTHERS** leaping/snapping fingers/yee-haaing/flicking lighters in fifty-gallon cowboy hats/mirrored contact lenses.)

CARNE BROTHERS
(In unison—metallic spaceman voice.)
Sheeeeriff Faaaaaaarbeeeeeen, preeeepaaaaare to deeefeeeeend yoooour-seeeeeelf!

Music: Swells.

(Enter right **GIRLS**, spinning in fringed, sequined leotards with miniature ponies strapped to tap shoes.)

GIRLS
(Sing)
Keep your hand on your gun!

(Enter left **BOYS**, slithering in polyurethane horse-head masks and air-fern thongs.)
BOYS
(Sing.)
Don't you trust anyone!

BOYS and GIRLS
(Form equilateral triangle/Charleston.)
There's just one kind of man
who tells the truth—
that's a dead man!

RED

(Backflips center, candy shoots out of his sleeves.)
(Sings.)
> *Or a gringo like me!*

WHORES

(Enter center in can-can.)
> *Don't be a fool for a smile or a kiss*
> *or your bullet might miss!*

BOYS, GIRLS, WHORES

(Form shape of optometrist seen from above: when dancers open legs in unison, optometrist changes to an eye chart. Close legs: optometrist. Open legs: eye chart.)
> *Keep your eye on your goal!*

CARNE BROTHERS

(Chase **BOYS, GIRLS, WHORES** away/lie down in their place and form Aztec calendar/rotate through seasons/invent the game of basketball with severed heads/play keep-away.)

Music: Harlem Globetrotter's Theme.

ALL

> *There's only one way to save you your life!*
> *It's a hand on your knife!*
> *And the devil in your soul!*

Music: Whirlwind orchestra, then one peppy, klezmerish clarinet.

ROSEY FARBEN

(Opens window in sky upper left, sticks bonneted head out, sings sweetly.)
> *Red, my love, it's dinner time,*
> *And I made enchilaaaa-das!*

RED

(Hands off severed head to **WHORE**, responds in kind.)
> *My faaaave-rit!*

(Exit **RED** humming happily. Warm, homey smell of **CHICKEN ENCHI-LADAS**, cilantro, sour cream, etc. seen from above.)

(Curtain.)

II.

"We're here because we're here because we're here because we're here.
We're here because we're here because we're here because we're here."

"We're Here Because We're Here"

Waiting with the Dead

Ten thousand people died last night in a Nicaraguan earthquake.
That's more than on the Titanic,
but less than in the Civil War.

If you lined up 10,000 dead people from head to toe,
would the bodies stretch from Maine to Florida,
or only from Maine to New Hampshire?

Which one would you rather hear on the news:
The dead stretched from North Dakota to Nebraska.
or *The dead stretched from Disneyland to Disneyworld?*

One out of every 300 people has murdered someone,
so if you were at a baseball game
and the stadium held 18,000 people,
there would be 60 murderers in the crowd.

If every one of those 60 murderers
murdered 299 people apiece,
there would be 17,940 dead people in the stadium.

With the help of both teams and the 60 murderers,
you could arrange the dead, head to toe,
to spell out words
so big they could only be read from the air.

Words like HELP
Or FUCK
Or there's always Gene Hackman's final words in *The Poseidon Adventure*:
HOW MANY MORE LIVES?

After that, you could all relax—
maybe grab a bite from the snack bar.
Make sure to keep a few players standing up,
waving their bright-colored caps back and forth,
just in case a rescue plane flies by.

WHY WE CAME AND WHY WE STAYED

No mystery there—we needed the dough.
It was 1956, and door-to-door salesmen
gigs were tougher to come by than dodos.
Sally'd always been a twitchy thing—and I loved it
in bed, but even before the caretaker chained the gate,
she was wincing and whimpering anytime
an ember went pop in the always-roaring fireplace—
in broad daylight yet—it was then somehow I knew
my white-gloved, bird-boned, wide-eyed wife was
a goner. Maybe I'd known all along—years before
we'd loosened the big red blob of wax
with its stamped-in thorny X holding the invitation's tongue down—
definitely by the time our host pulled a no-show at dinner
and sent, as a stand-in, "his deepest regrets." OK
so I knew, and said, "You sleep with the girls tonight, darling—

you'll be safer that way." I knew all along
and now we all know "Someone's Got to Pay"
was that prom's theme, but Sally, poor kid,
never knew her dad'd even driven a school bus,
much less drunk, off a cliff, and killed thirty-two kids.
A lot of people hated her, I know that too,
but do you know why she shrieked and flopped around
like that? Because *Life* told her life was a straight line
leading off the 405 to a split-level ranch house in Van Nuys
but *Life* lied—about everything: how it looked,
the stuff inside, my name, her name, but especially
the address, which turned out to be at the end
of a long red hallway lined with stuffed, hunted heads.
All we gave ol' Sal to help find her way back
from the bathroom was a cheapo sputtering flashlight
and one super doozy of a nightie.

WE ARE AFRAID

We are afraid of Godzilla movies
and the Japanese people who made them.
What do they have against us anyway? We are afraid
of spontaneously combusting: drunk, alone and nowhere
near a fireplace and the only thing left will be from the knees
on down. We are afraid
of Carpal Tunnel Syndrome. We are afraid
of the thing on the wing of the plane. We are afraid
the peeping tom had a damn good reason to pick
our window over the neighbor's. We are afraid
an elderly couple will kidnap us and keep us locked in a box
under their bed for ten years, opening it every other day
to spoon feed us pudding and they'll never change
our diaper and when finally they tire of us
stinking up the place they'll take us out
to the woods and let us go but we won't know what to do so we'll
find our way back and they'll say *Lord have mercy*
and use every last ounce of their elderly strength
to beat us unconscious, then they'll put us back in the box. We are afraid
of junior high school students and the nauseating things
they say among their own kind. We are afraid
of getting needles in our eyes. We are afraid
of what's in the Tupperware. We are afraid
when we get old we'll be shipped off to an island
for people who spent all their money on beer. We are afraid
of our own unborn children—that one day it'll all come down
to *Mom, Dad—can I have the car tonight?* and when we say
no they'll shoot us in the head. We are afraid
of Mississippi. We are afraid
the frogs will disappear. We are afraid
glaciers at both ends of the planet will melt and everyone left alive will be
"escorted" to the Yukon Territories and we'll pass the time
not teaching the kids how to fish
not planting corn in a biosphere
not writing books about starting over or what the fuck went wrong, instead
we'll run around just as screwy
as we were before the thaw—still selfish, still whiny, still cowering
like beat down dogs before the voice in our heads—
you're small you're slow you suckers suck—a voice
harder to kill off than roaches—a voice
that ain't afraid of shit.

A Common American Name

It's December, there's a blizzard,
and I'm going swimming at the Greenpoint Y.
Five young African men in scuffed down vests
huddle in the hallway around an old vending machine
while the receptionist punches the buttons and yanks the knobs.
There's nothing left in there but licorice ropes and Lifesavers,
and not until I'm squeezing by do I notice the men
have no forearms—nothing from the elbows down.
"Have a great swim, Jen!" she calls to me,
wide-eyed as a hostage, her voice high and tight—
the same woman who normally no more than grunts
when I walk by—who has never called my name before.
I know hers too—it's also Jen (short for *Jennifer*,
a Welsh form of *Guinevere* meaning pure, white wave).

SAMURAI AND CHILD

The child still follows me.
Float away, butterfly, were the only words
I spoke to him among the burning huts that day
yet he has dragged his bad foot behind
my horse for weeks through these mountains,
sometimes dropping out to lap at a stream
or shove handfuls of grass
into his brown, rotten mouth.
But I always find him
in the morning near the fire.

It will be winter soon. Does he know?
He is dumb—or crazy. The sounds
when he trips echo sharply
like the caws of crows after an ice storm
but I've grown to know his sounds.
My grandmother, too, had a clubfoot—
and her own mother nearly drowned her
in a bucket at birth for it.

The boy believes I cannot die.
When I do, hopefully
he will have the sense
to steal the coins from my purse,
wrap himself in my yukatta
and eat me—not the horse.

MASTERING THE LESSON OF ODDS

Congratulations, Uncle George, but one good day
at the dog track and a yo-yo don't make candy
for dinner OK. Muncie Man stopped by today he did
and hissed all red face through the deadbolt:
"Georgie's waltzed his last one, kid." So no duh
you're already planning to sneak out and leave us
all night alone again but Mom gave you fifty bucks
to babysit and buy groceries plus you promised:
"No horseshit I swear to fucking Christ this time, Irene."
But fourteen years I've heard you blah blah blah.
Reading you's like reading in a car: all that jumping around
gives me a headache. You even run like chickenshit
and you'll never be anything but the same big pussy
what fucked up all our birthday parties: showing up wasted,
shaky and late, blubbering into your five-dollar steak—you,
your Prince Valiant haircut and them sissy-ass, baby blue pants.

Seizing the Li'l Miss Universe

Father and I were snorkeling through a school of barracuda
who couldn't take their filmy eyes off us:
our long, tanned legs waving like sea grass,
the veins on our arms, blue as coral...
I couldn't change direction as quick as the fish,
but I could bench-press my own weight in bricks.

Father had been a spotter for Jack LaLanne years back—
before Jack ate Styrofoam on cable TV.
A rough home life, Jack's dad called him Judy,
his mom called him Jack-off,
and his granddad called him Pansy Boy.
Jack told Father *I can't blame my family.*
Growing up in Florida like that
where inflated pig bladders passed for balloons,
and they pulled their own teeth out with pliers.

But injustice stuck on Dad like a bad duck dinner;
he'd never suffer a bully, nor a hicky Floridian.
My back pressed to the bench, he would rant over me
and forget all the weight I was pressing:
What if every boy called Judy took up Kung Fu,
bought a gun, and came home hell-bent for leather?
Then what about their Goddamn orange groves?

That'd be one tall can
of sunshiny whoop-ass
was always the safest reply.

He spoke as if the reckoning were eons away,
as if the human brain would have to rearrange
itself first, undergo some great tectonic shift
before Judy boys would dare take out
the Everglades in a hail of jujitsu and Uzis.

Down there amongst the occasional clown fish,
I wasn't thinking about any of this.
Father had crawled back into the boat
and was oiling himself up shiny as a mirror.

I was thinking about buying a bra,
and especially my wisdom teeth, how they were
coming in, and I was praying Father would be
gentle this time—but if not,
please, God, give me Novocaine.

MY BIG GERMAN BRA

"Shut up and listen! Sit up
straight and stop simpering!
You call this supper?!
We wouldn't throw such food
to a dog in Berkenboorgsen!
I elbow you out of my way with a *harumpf!*
You call this a building?!?! Bah!
Your arms are full of schokolade!
My legs! They burst mit iodine!
Idjots! You know nothing
of crafting fine hood ornaments:
Silver women mit blondes hair
heaving their metal bosoms to the wind!
Anchored down mit tight, wide straps!"

Dr. Langzahne, DDS, Sees His Shadow

The Doctor darts out into oncoming traffic
and I'm left behind, toes gripping the curb
                            as usual. *COME ON!* he starts
in with his back to me, still dodging
honking cars
                COME ON YOU SEE-THROUGH PUSSY COME ON!
I pretend like I can't hear him, shirk
and point at my ear, but he reaches the other side
and turns those jumpy, bloodshot eyes on me,
fists clenched like a pissed-off kid, so torqued up
he can't see the traffic between us

and so I begin: Being a dentist is—
                BANGOHOWDYDOODIEBOYOH!
Teeth are like—
        TREES!
Dentistry is like—
           PERFORMING A VEIN GRAFT ON A TRAMPOLINE!
(I gave him that one) You are—
                EL MUCHO MACHO BOCO GRANDE!
You're smoking—
        VICODIN! I'M SMOKING VICODIN!
(At this point, I'm supposed to join in)
We're smoking Vicodin—
              I'M SMOKING VICODIN!
Leeeeeeet's goooooooo—
           SWIMMING!

It's actually kind of cute the way he
hurls both hands in the air on that one,
his fingers splayed out, all Bob Fosse happy hands.

Who's the guy who's cavity free?—
              I AM! I AM!
Who's got the sexiest drill in town?—
             I DO! I DO!
Are you strong?—
          LISTEN BUB, I'VE GOT RADIOACTIVE BLOOD!
Gumming the roast beef's a pity—
           BOO HOO!

This time when he makes the boo-hoo face, it occurs
to me that, under different circumstances,
the Doctor might've been a truly great actor:
he believes in the words coming out
of his mouth. So did Elvis.

The light changes and he takes off.
One day I'll get creamed by a truck
and he'll be miles away. But I don't mind
the act so much. At least we're outside.
After fifteen hours under the fluorescents,
he tends to forget I'm alive.

Fiancée: Hot, and à la Mode

I'm a pretty little peach pie
with a honking chunk cut out

and though I've begged you: *Lean*
on my crust, both crimped and egg-washed—

your full weight! and together we'll
foil all those tacky rebels spazzing off

with action figures (mint) in the Altstadtplatz:
our brimming packs of Camels,

our demeanor: Dean Martin, and altogether far—
I know that you know that I know

your foot'd smoosh right though
my heart of lard, my wet Kleenex back

bone, and that "cooling racks" are code
for a hot air balloon full o' fibs.

When I order you: *Lay*
it on me, Brucey! can you see,

through my drippy window and out
the other side, me: some day-

old blood pudding: half-
off, in drag, eating

its self?

CHICKEN BUCKET

Today I turn thirteen and quit the 4-H club for good.
I smoke way too much pot for that shit.
Besides, Mama lost the rabbit and both legs
from the hip down in Vegas.
What am I supposed to do? Pretend to have a rabbit?
Bring an empty cage to the fair and say,
His name's REO Speedwagon and he weighs eight pounds?
My teacher, Mr. Ortiz says, *I'll miss you, Cassie,*
then he gives me a dime of free crank and we have sex.
I do up the crank with Mama and her boyfriend, Rick.
She throws me the keys to her wheelchair and says,
Baby, go get us a chicken bucket.
So I go and get us a chicken bucket.
On the way back to the trailer, I stop at Hardy's liquor store.
I don't want to look like a dork
carrying a chicken bucket into the store—
and even though Mama always says,
Never leave chicken where someone could steal it—
I wrap my jacket around it and hide it
under the wheelchair in the parking lot.
I've got a fake ID says my name's Sherry and I'm 22,
so I pick up a gallon of Montezuma tequila,
a box of Whip-Its and four pornos.
Mama says, *That Jerry Butler's got a real wide dick.*
But the whole time I'm in line, I'm thinking,
Please God let the chicken bucket be OK.
Please God let the chicken bucket be OK.
Please God let the chicken bucket be OK.
The guy behind me's wearing a T-shirt
that says, *Mustache Rides 10¢.*
So I say, *All I got's a nickel.*
He says, *You're cute,*
so we go out to his van and have sex.
His dick's OK, but I've seen wider.
We drink most of the tequila and I ask him,
Want a Whip-It?
He says, *Fuck no—that shit rots your brain.*
And when he says that, I feel kind of stupid
doing another one. But then I remember

what Mama always told me:
Baby be your own person.
Well fuck yes.
So I do another Whip-It,
all by myself and it is great.
Suddenly it hits me—
Oh shit! the chicken bucket!
Sure enough, it's gone.
Mama's going to kill me.
Those motherfuckers even took my jacket.
I can't buy a new chicken bucket
because I spent all the money at Hardy's.
So I go back to the trailer, crouch outside
behind a bush, do all the Whip-Its,
puke on myself, roll in the dirt,
and throw open the screen door like a big empty wind.
Mama! Some Mexicans jumped me!
They got the chicken bucket,
plus the rest of the money!

I look around the trailer.
Someone's taken all my old stuffed animals
and Barbies and torn them to pieces.
Fluff and arms and heads are all over the place.
I say someone did it,
but the only person around is Rick.
Mama is nowhere to be seen.
He cracks open another beer and says,
What chicken bucket?

Well, that was a long a time ago.
Rick and I got married
and we live in a trailer in Boron.
We don't live in a trailer park though—
in fact there's not another house around
for miles. But the baby keeps me
company. Rick says I'm becoming
quite a woman, and he's going to let Mama know that
if we ever see her again.

Found Poem: Ol' Dirty Bastard on Visitors

People. People when they want to get in
touch with me now. You know bein'

in New York you know I mean every day
somebody's at my fuckin' house you know

what I'm sayin'? I live with my Momma and
shit you know? Momma she ain't got no

privacy. Every day it's her cousin
over there spendin' the night or some shit.

•

I'm here now
[LA].

You got to travel three thousand fuckin' miles to see
me you know and they still

comin'. Ain't that some shit?
They still comin' but they got to go

the fuck home. I'm a do it like Jim Jones
did. I'm a get all of them to come and visit me

and they gonna get a one-way ticket
you know what I'm sayin'?

LOOKING FOR THE CITY

After the cans run out
and Sylvia keeps asking
what are we going to eat when the cans run out?
don't tell her the cans ran out
even though she keeps asking
even though you're sick
of her and you want to push her down
or push a handful of grass into her
tiny mouth don't do it because people never push
food into a person they love
even if the grass tastes OK to you
better than nothing and you're bigger
than she is and she's sick because she only eats
cans don't do it do something else

like take a long walk up the hill
to the trailer where the rabbits live
they're soft but don't eat them
because they belong to the man
who lives inside the trailer
somehow they survived
he says the city was awful the people
got what they deserved forget
about it and then
don't eat my rabbits

or try reading a comic book
this one's my favorite
Wonder Woman is wonderful
she lives in the city and makes people tell the truth
with her shiny gold lasso too bad
you can't tell Sylvia the truth
Sylvia get ready to eat
grass when the cans run out
because Sylvia keeps asking
what are we going to eat when the cans run out?
or maybe she's not moving at all anymore

so carry her to the trailer
and lay her on the mattress inside
and the comic books too it's all
you got it's not your trailer
those aren't your rabbits say stupid
empty cans and light a match
people have to eat all sorts of things
in the city and when you're walking
a new way away thinking I
love you Sylvia ask the man
what will happen to the rabbits
and he'll say there is
everything everywhere.

III.

"Take care of thyself, gentle Yahoo."

Jonathan Swift

And Now a Message from the Sea Horses Whinnying in Our Mailbags

Welcome back to the show.
We've received hundreds of letters
about sea horses lately. Here's one
from Violet Finch of Whistlepip:

Dear Morning Show, are sea horses
fish, or something
else? Sometimes they
look like birds—
or seeds!

Well, Violet, these vulnerable vertebrates
don't grow on trees, but they tend to
drift like fluff from a blown dandelion—
or a gingko pod (but odorless);
they do peck and/or nibble—
depending on the fibrousness
of the reeds around them.

Maxwell Toother in Regina writes: *Where*
does a sea horse come from?
Is there such a thing
as sea horse caviar,
can I
eat it,
will it
taste good?

Sea horses begin their lives as dust
collecting on the spinning skin
of foamy ocean bubbles, so sorry,
Max, you cannot eat their eggs.
After the inevitable pop, they take on
myriad shapes: all silent, but surprisingly
tough, and not a delicious one
in the bunch.

From Rusty Frame in Whitecloud:
Hello, please tell me how

my kid knows what a sea horse
is? She's only two;
she's never visited the zoo,
still she yammers all day long.
P.S. and why can't I remember
what a sea horse looks
like?

The sea horse is inside us, Rusty—
so the saying goes. Kids love 'em!
They're the new dinosaurs,
but before you buy, mind
you they thrive amidst quiet companions:
gray gobies, etc., and the tank
must be brackish enough
to obscure such specimens
as the ghostly ghost
pipefish and leafy sea dragon's
visible heartbeats, their inscrutable
comings and goings.

A Bedtime Story for Puff

We haven't always lived in the trees, kitty—
tucked up like pill bugs between layers of moss.
Back in the desert, we serpentined
from stone to stone, huddled under
their muddy undersides, bathed in troughs
of corralled sheep. Vinegarroons abounded
and awayed with our hen eggs. Dust
on the outside and the in, we were edgeless.
Sure, we scrounged our share of shiny bits:
an abandoned couch sprung open like a watch,
a blue hat gone tan under the wide, white sun.
You'd have hated it, kitty—no leaves
to hide behind. Nothing to swat at.

But then again, vast savannas are sliding
somewhere along the skin of your cells...
Perhaps you would've loved to track
approaching sandstorms (they'd take sweet
time climbing over the wide horizon)
or the scent of a single roadrunner woven
into the big, heavy blanket of blank smells.
There were no surprises.

You were just a dust mote then, a tabby-
striped wisp asleep on the lips
of these bright red flowers,
dreaming fat rabbits:
a sneaky, orange, unrepentant eye.

THE ROLE OF TAFFY

After the huffing mishap and his fifth hernia surgery,
the insurance company refused to cover the aging Austrian action star,
despite an elaborately Swiss-engineered truss belt.
Over budget and heavily medicated, the producer
got a black Lab named Taffy to stand in for all the physical stuff.
Fucking Christ people love dogs, he told the crew.
No one told him it was a stupid idea. Outside the barbed,
golden studio gates, the rest of us pushed shopping carts
and sucked on old Styrofoam Burger King boxes.
We wondered what the words meant on various canned goods,
and it was always a great time for fire.

The film was a smash: throughout the monsoons we stood up
to our knees in muddy fields and watched shiny Taffy flicker
on a screen of dirty sheets: doing ninja numchuck stuff,
smoking big cigars, making love to dancers dressed like cupcakes.
No one said, *That's not what's-his-name! That's a dog!*
We taped posters of the animal to our carts and said,
Taffy! Taffy! Taffy! because there were no magazines.
But the placid Lab, who'd never believed in God, only Heaven,
declined the studio's offers of clipped ears and speech therapy—
instead decided to join the aging Austrian action star
at his stately home hanging over the canyon
where she'd pace a wide perimeter
around his big, disassembling body,
sniff her dish, watch the door, wait for wolves.

Famed Psychic Gardener Flits Through, Gives Tips

In light of the upcoming time change,
she dropped by with bunches of tulips:
one red with gold, one orange with green;
both showy and obviously French.

She was always doing stuff like that:
tornado sirens hooing away
and she's off looting blue peonies,
or tying sage to my tabby's tail
to ward off dogs and bouts of ennui.

Parties, parties, parties, and parties…
yet she kept her fluids up, brought down
white birdies sailing o'er the great

white net. I asked her about my peas:
to freeze them or let them get greener?
to fry them with onions in oil
or steam them? She asked, "Do you hear that?

it's the sound of your pods ripening.
Let their zippers tell you how to do."

But what of my orchids? Should I splice
prize-winning Guatemalan Green Squids
with novice Australian Cat Faces?
"Jauntiest kings of deception, bad

flowers, the *epidendrum cochleatum*
and *diuris filifolia*.
These emit pheromones, read our minds.
Encourage not their waxy, forked tongues."

Gesturing to the tree beyond the wall
I asked, what kind—with its giant blooms
pink as pussycats inside and white
at the tips of its petals? "Go now,"

she said, "and bury some fish beneath
its webby black canopy—golden
ones, still with eyes—oily carp or koi."

WILLARD, I APOLOGIZE

for laughing all these years
you've wished the centenarians
Happy Birthday.
I was wrong.
I thought I'd never die.

But lately I can't hear you
say the names (*Bettina Swoop*
from St. Paul, MN, turns 103 today—
and what a pretty lady!)
without crying like a baby.

ANOTHER MOTIVE FOR METAPHOR

I love to masturbate, especially
after a poem of mine's accepted in
a literary magazine. Shit—
I open up that letter, smile awhile
and think, "This one goes out to Don, a total
tool who I temped for in '89:
data-mother-fucking-entry *this*.
Whose got 'inappropriate footwear' now?
The inappropriate footwear's on the other
foot today, you hick," I tell him, tell
them all, as, lifting up my shirt, I notice
nipples! Mine (O, gorgeous areolas!—
pink as peonies)! And ass (my bouncy
pony, prance in skintight smarty pants!)!

SAGA OF THE HIPPY SCI-FI HOMOSEXUAL

Hippy Sci-Fi Homosexual's got a line on the ultra mild
Taiwanese pop rocks—they're ideal for a low-carb cold sore.
Hippy Sci-Fi Homosexual's so happy he could crap
about his new pair of fringy boots he traded
Big Dick Richard a pudding cup for.
Hippy Sci-Fi Homosexual's got a bathrobe named Ol' Chickenshit.
For Hippy Sci-Fi Homosexual's lunchie-wunch's always
two tuna schooners, green peas in heavy syrup, and a root beer Big Gulp
jammed down each rainbow leg warmer.
Hippy Sci-Fi Homosexual's a BIIIG FAAAN OF PUUURL JAAAM.
Hippy Sci-Fi Homosexual believes
if you're giving it away for free, it must be good!
Hippy Sci-Fi Homosexual's gifts are always handmade
and incorporate rocks and leaves.
Hippy Sci-Fi Homosexual took a kitten home
from K-Mart and damn if that kitten didn't wind up right back there.
Many years ago Hippy Sci-Fi Homosexual played Dr. Goldfoot
in *Dr. Goldfoot and the Bikini Machine.*
Now he won't stop singing the song:
"Dah-kter Goldfuh-huuut…an the bahkini muhsheen!"

Someone once wished ass cancer upon Hippy Sci-Fi Homosexual.
Well go screw, jealous buttmunch!
Hippy Sci-Fi Homosexual's not going down without a fight
or some pills. Hippy Sci-Fi Homosexual's got his neon half-socks
and the half-life of neon…but Hippy Sci-Fi Homosexual is a little scared
he'll wind up looking like Julia Child—giant hunchback monster
with arms coming out his ears, chopping up animal face
with a voice like a helium-filled hippo puppet…
but Hippy Sci-Fi Homosexual isn't that much scared because
Hippy Sci-Fi Homosexual's running System 69,
Hippy Sci-Fi Homosexual's got the Robo DM going WOOWOOWOO,
Hippy Sci-Fi Homosexual will envivo pronto all over your el baño.
Hippy Sci-Fi Homosexual always says *"Hi Heather"*
when he sees her being dragged through the park by a big dog on a leash
but Heather doesn't have a dog, man!
And if there's one thing Hippy Sci-Fi Homosexual knows for sure
is that chick's not *even* Heather.

THE BEST THANKSGIVING EVER

After the meal, Sandy decided we should spice up charades
by slapping the loser's butt with a ping-pong paddle.
Whenever Ed got slapped, he farted because he was so nervous.
The ladies won, slapped all the men's butts, but then what to do?
"Take off your clothes!" I told Sean, who didn't seem like the kind
of guy who'd do such a thing—but he was, and he did. Then Jim
took off his clothes. And then John. Then the other Jim
who brought all the lovely bottles of wine. And finally Ed.
Deb came out of the bathroom and saw five big men naked in the kitchen.
They screamed, "Take off your clothes!" We all figured she would,
and she did. Then Sandy the Slapmaster, then me, then Tomoko
who kept her glasses on. We walked around the house naked,
talking about how it was to be naked with other naked people,
how none of the guys had boners, and how cold it was out in the garage.
Somebody found a big bottle of vodka. We made a no-hugging rule.
John kept trying to open the curtains and show the neighbors
what they were missing. Deb thought an orgy was imminent,
but since we'd all spent a lot of time in Iowa, I didn't think it would fly.
Jim passed out. Ed put a robe on. I passed out. We woke up
the next morning in T-shirts, ate bagels from Bagel Land, and said,
"We all got naked last night." That afternoon, on our way
to the Walt Whitman Mall, the ladies gave each other nicknames
ending with the word Bitch. Deb was Shy Bitch,
Sandy was Gentle Bitch, Tomoko was Slutty Bitch and I was Silent Bitch.
All the bitches agreed that slapping people's butts with a paddle
was something we needed to do every weekend, that this was the best
Thanksgiving ever, and that Ed had the biggest dick we'd ever seen.

ODE TO THE NEW GIRL AT THE OFFICE

O new girl at the office!
How many young girls I've watched come and go afore ye
in their itty-bitty Charlie's Angels T-shirts, the shit-
brown trim around the neck and sleeves like donkeys' halos, and O!
shiny tennis shoes with soles sproingy as bubble baths. How the body
glitter settles in the creases of your eyelids like electric sand!
You are a whirling calliope of daisiness, new girl at the office!

O new girl at the office, I pity you sitting
at the usually empty desk with nothing
but salt and sporks in your drawers! Lo! Nary a pencil
with which to write how much you hate it here, over and over, in Spanish,
French or whatever language you studied in high school. Nary a clock
on the wall to show how time's passing
slower than the black
Costclub coffee
in the pot
evap-
orat-
ing.

O new girl at the office! By the time I learn your name you will be
gone so I will call you Yorbalinda!
O Yorbalinda! You are too pink for these beige walls. And by the time
I hear you groan through the partition, groan to no one in particular,
"God, it's so quiet in here!" you will already be fading
like strawberry perfume from the stale air around us.

Run, Yorbalinda, run!
As fast as you can!
And don't look back!
Home! to your friends with patchwork skirts over their bell bottom jeans
and tight Space 1999 ski jackets, for at this very moment they are
discovering the wonders of psychedelic drugs!
Home! to your music going *dooosha-dooosha-dooosha-dooosha.*
Turn it up loud for us, Yorbalinda.
We, who are beyond boredom and already dead
wish you well at the next temp job

where you'll forget all our names, Yorbalinda,
but our blank, hollow eyes
will haunt you e'er long.

FREESTYLE VAGINA/"FREE VAGINA!" STYLE

bird bird
> *daddy daddy*

bird bird
> *daddy daddy*

> > *bird—*

i call my pussy a pussy
'cause it's like a cat:
it never comes when you call it

bird bird
> *daddy daddy*

> > *bird—*

i call my pussy a pussy
'cause it's like a cat:
it spends "a lot of time" in the litterbox
mulling over the nuances of its own shit

a lot of time
a lot of rhyme
in the box
never stop talking
about my pussy-socks

my pussy's like a jewelry box
full of breakfast cereal
captain crunch
is the only man in this poem
but he's really
in my pussy

bird bird
> *daddy daddy*

> > *fire—*

my pussy's a piñata on fire
at a little mexican kid's birthday party
don't run, josé—
my pussy will not hurt you
'cause you are an innocent child,

like i was once long before…
don't run, josé!
please! OK, really
don't run 'cause it probably *will* hurt you
if you run, so stop running
and put the cake down—s l o w l y
deja la torte, josé!

avé avé

       papi papi

              fuego—

my pussy
is no wussy
or a sissy
don't you kiss me
on my mouth
'cause i'm talking
kiss my pussy
it's got chapstick
in it's knapsack
and it goes quack
when you kiss it
pack a sack lunch
i've a got a hunch
that my pussy
will be going
on a picnic
very soon

       very soon

             to the moon

                   oo the moon

and then i will fly
to meet greet squeeze the feet of my sisters
who are practically chickens
stuffed with eggs and periods
while drag queens get all the good semicolons;

THE OPPOSITE OF CRUNCHBERRIES

The opposite of Crunchberries is
fried chicken.
The opposite of fried chicken is
geometry class.
The opposite of geometry class is
an otter.
The opposite of an otter is
William Shatner.
The opposite of William Shatner is
the Mardi Gras.
The opposite of the Mardi Gras is
Nazis.
The opposite of Nazis is
Jello-wrestling for children.
The opposite of Jello-wrestling for children is
a BB gun.
The opposite of a BB gun is
a used fabric softener sheet.
The opposite of a used fabric softener sheet is
a prison warden.
The opposite of a prison warden is
an Easter egg.
The opposite of an Easter egg is
old lunchmeat.
The opposite of old lunchmeat is
a geisha girl
who's wearing a kimono
covered in bright pink Crunchberries.

COME HOME, SNOOPI
For a Balinese Dog

Snoopi, you're a puppy eclipsed
by big Taro's brave bounce
between the tall green rows of rice.
But you stick to it, keep right on chasing

his shadow, clueless he gave up
hours ago on the ducks and loped back
to the porch for a snooze. This morning
as you yapped at a garter snake,

you missed your chance at toast and jam.
Taro got some, even the two sneaky cats.
Snoopi, figure out it's hot, and now's not
the time for sticking your nose in an ant hill

or pestering dumb carp in the pond. Sure
no one thinks much of you yet—
only that you're goofy
rolling around under the lime tree,

muu-muued Ibu shoos you with the broom...
but Taro's getting older—
(see the gray hairs on his muzzle?)
we all are, kid, and one day we'll squeal

your name: *O Snoopi! come save us*
from the rats with their grabby pink hands!
You'll be grateful for a little shade then
and your twitchless dreams will ring

with human words, *good dog*, and sweets.

Freckles.

I can tell your shoulder
from the back
of your hand
from your knee
by the hue,
circumference,
and the distance between.

Like a map
of all the sun
that ever fell
on your body.

THE BRIGHT LIGHT OF RESPONSIBILITY

My friend said, "Let's go down to the river.
Bosses from all over the state are having sex with their young secretaries
in a wild group fucking kind of office thing with prosthetics and electricity.
They're misusing whipped cream can chargers and animal sedatives.
The press is invited and nobody's going to get in trouble."
I told her, "No! I won't go! It's not right!
Even if these big fat men get interviewed on *Entertainment Tonight*
and they never get in trouble and this fancy paparazzi rimjob propels
every hoochie mama participant into some star studded modeling career,
it's still not right!
Getting on top of someone in public is wrong."
So my friend said, "OK. Let's go crazy and not shower for a month.
Then we get on the city bus for $1.35 and wet our pants.
It'll smell terrible and make people incredibly nervous,
but no one will ask us any questions and we won't get in trouble."
Well, I told her, "Hey, no! It's not right!
God invented hygiene to serve mankind.
Urine belongs inside of you, not slopping around on public transportation.
No one would ask you any questions
because talking to someone who wets their pants on a city bus
is like talking to a space invader from Mars.
People are afraid you might flick pee at them or something
and ruin their lives." Then my friend said,
"Well OK Miss God-Almighty-Hot-Pants-Goes-to-Church,
what say we give up regular food like macaroni and tomatoes,
forget we ever ate them, and concentrate on vending machines:
your Funyuns, your Mellow Yellow, your Tootsie Rolls
your Cherry Pepsi, your Now 'N' Laters, your Pepperoni Combos.
We eat nothing but that for the entirety of our formative years
and well into adulthood. Then we complain about our teeth,
how they're all rotten, and lift up our lips to show our coworkers the holes.
Then we buy some guns.
We force European tourists at gun point
to look at our holes. Then we say, 'We don't care.
We'll just get them all pulled out,' and we won't get in trouble, OK?"
I told her, "OK my eye! It is not OK! It's not right!
The four food groups are for everybody.
Vegetables are not optional.
You cannot substitute Pringles for rice.

People!! All teeth start out just fine
and then you go and fill them full of holes.
It's not like a car accident!
A person drives all the cars in the city that is their mouth.
You build the roads. You elect the public officials
and they will even wear what you tell them to wear.
If you really like stupid silver platform boots and empire waist baby doll dresses
then that is what the mayor will wear to his inaugural dinner
and every day for the rest of his life.
It's all yours and leaving non-English speakers free
to wander around in rental cars,
up to God knows what kind of crap, unchecked, is madness!
Forget it. I know: let's go get ten of those big green tropical cocktails
and see who can drink theirs the fastest.
I'll drive."
"OK," she said
and together we walked out into the bright light of responsibility.

Instinct in the Age of Astrology

(Curtain up on spotlit café table and two chairs, surrounded by darkness.)

(Enter **CAPABLE GOLDEN RETRIEVER** right on hind legs. He looks around to make sure he's in the right place, sits, takes out Collins' *Apes, Men & Language* and begins reading.)

(Enter **ENTHUSIASTIC NEWFOUNDLAND**, left, also on hind legs, wearing an enthusiastic hat, carrying a well worn copy of Dinesen's *Seven Gothic Tales*. She sees **RETRIEVER**, smiles widely and scrambles onto small chair opposite.)

NEWFIE
Hi!

RETRIEVER
(Lays down *Apes* and smiles.)
    Hello!

(The two sniff each other's books.)

NEWFIE
How was talking today?

RETRIEVER
Sometimes I wish I didn't.

NEWFIE
In Mexico, they speak Spanish.

(More sniffing each other's books.)

RETRIEVER
But they'd expect you to speak Spanish eventually.

NEWFIE
(With exaggerated smile.)
    Not if you smile a lot!

(The two sniff their own books awhile.)

RETRIEVER

(Suddenly.)
    Hey! Look what I liked doing today!

(**RETRIEVER** stands and begins scratching floor rhythmically with back paws like a chicken.)

NEWFIE

(Looking on appreciatively.)
    What does it mean?

RETRIEVER

    I don't know, but it's really fun.
(Sings.)
    I don't know. I don't get it. I don't know. I don't get it…

NEWFIE

(Joins him.)
    I don't know. I don't get it. I don't know…

(8 minutes.)

(**BOTH** flop back into their chairs and laugh.)

(10 minutes.)

(**RETRIEVER** reaches into darkness off stage, pulls out ashtray, lights up, smiles.)

(**NEWFIE** sniffs the air, licks a crumb off the tablecloth, sighs.)

RETRIEVER

    What's wrong?

(Pause.)

NEWFIE

    I read our horoscopes today.

RETRIEVER

(Exasperated, throws up paws.)
    Why do you keep reading those things?!?

NEWFIE

(Lower lip quivering.)

They said that your character was modeled after the great shysters, like P. T. Barnum and Sister Aimee Semple McPherson and that one day you'd retire to a circus museum in upstate Wisconsin...

(Tears up, hides head in paws, then continues.)

...but they said I was modeled after Jesus—that I knew too much—and I had to die!

(Bursts into tears.)

RETRIEVER

(Places paw on her shoulder.)

Darling, all horoscopes were originally created during the Civil War—just like shoe sizes. We're simply too lazy to write new ones.

(**NEWFIE** relieved, uncovers face, smiles hesitantly.)

RETRIEVER

(Petting her head.)

I tell you the exact same thing, every day.

BOTH

(Smile into each other's faces, join paws, rise, walk front center, wave to audience floppily, sincerely.)

Bye bye! Bye bye! Bye bye!...

(18 minutes.)

(Curtain down.)

ACKNOWLEDGMENTS

Thanks to the anthologies, journals and websites in which these poems have appeared:

Another Chicago Magazine: Dr. Langzahne, DDS, Sees His Shadow; *Mighty, Mighty Primate: Reconsidered*; The Opposite of Crunchberries; The Role of Taffy

Barrow Street: Willard, I Apologize

Bellevue Literary Review: We Are Afraid

The Best American Erotic Poems: From 1800 to the Present: Another Motive for Metaphor

The Best American Poetry 1997: The Bright Light of Responsibility

The Best American Poetry 2003: Love Blooms at Chimsbury after the War

Black Warrior Review: Reticence in the Afterglow of a Powerfully Frisky Fit; And Now a Message from the Sea Horses Whinnying in Our Mailbags

The Brooklyn Rail: Waiting with the Dead

Coconut: A Bedtime Story for Puff

Columbia Poetry Review: A Common American Name; Famed Psychic Gardener Flits Through, Gives Tips

Fence: Instinct in the Age of Astrology

Field: Love Blooms at Chimsbury after the War

Forklift, Ohio: Distress Call from the Canyon

Free Radicals: American Poets Before Their First Books: Chicken Bucket; Cruising for Prostitutes; My Big German Bra

Great American Prose Poems: From Poe to Present: Hot Ass Poem

The Hat: Another Motive for Metaphor; The Odds of Probability in Levittown

LIT: Mastering the Lesson of Odds; Spring and Still Some Short; Why We Came and Why We Stayed

Painted Bride Quarterly: The Best Thanksgiving Ever; Found Poem: Ol' Dirty Bastard on Visitors

Ploughshares: The Origin of Stories in the Kingdom of Parrots

Prairie Schooner: Samurai and Child

Sad Little Breathings and Other Acts of Ventriloquism: Of the Flock

Shout New York: Avenue of the Americas; Hot Ass Poem

Somewhat: Saga of the Hippy Sci-Fi Homosexual

Spoon River: Seizing the Li'l Miss Universe; Fiancée: Hot, and á la Mode

Verse/POL: Of the Flock; Waiting with the Dead

Unpleasant Event Schedule: My Favorite Little Story

A Gringo Like Me takes its title from the song of the same name in *Gunfight at Red Sands*, 1963, directed by Ricardo Blasco. Words by C. Dannell, music by Ennio Morricone, performed by Peter Tavis.

Thank you Jody & Tom Knox, Marilyn McCormick, Kathleen Mann, Ada Limón, Kit & Joel McNally, James Valentine DuPratt, Gifford Hopkins, Marie Ponsot, Mark Doty, Alan Michael Parker, Daniel Nester, Shanna Compton, Deborah Stein & James Knudsen, Kelly Thomas, Cammie & Sarah Lulu and Scotty P. on Point, Liz Clappi, and all the nice people at the Midwestern Ocean Assc. of the United States of America HQ ("Do Whatever's Funner").

Photo credit: Alexa Vachon

Jennifer L. Knox was born in Lancaster, California—where absolutely anything can be made into a bong. Her poems have appeared in the anthologies *The Best American Poetry* (1997, 2003 and 2006), *Great American Prose Poems: From Poe to Present, Free Radicals: American Poets Before Their First Books*, and *The Best American Erotic Poems: From 1800 to the Present*. She has taught poetry writing at New York University and Hunter College, and is available for children's parties, séances, and tradeshow booth demonstrations. *A Gringo Like Me* is her first book. Her second book, a large print how-to titled *Drunk By Noon*, is also available from Bloof.

www.jenniferlknox.com

PRAISE FOR *A GRINGO LIKE ME*

"In her first go, this poet has given us one 'hot ass book ass' to admire for a good long time." —*Southeast Review*

"Knox's first book, *A Gringo Like Me*, reads more like Richard Pryor with a MFA. But for all the blue humor, there's real craft on display.... Knox has the ability to take a ridiculous situation and tell it in such a way that it seems real.... [She] doesn't back off, doesn't blink." —*Verse*

"Because she makes it look so easy, it's easy for the casual reader to ignore the strength and grace in the lines of Jennifer L. Knox's *A Gringo Like Me*, as she carries us from one fresh image to the next. By the second read, it grows clear that a deep understanding of form and prosody underlies what are crafted to resemble poems of loose spontaneity."
—*The Columbia Journal of American Studies*

"Only a couple of times a year do I truly get excited about a book of poetry. Jennifer L. Knox's *A Gringo Like Me* is one of these rare gems. While reading it I kept thinking, I can't believe this is poetry." —*Powells.com*

Made in the USA
Lexington, KY
31 October 2012